TITAN BOOKS

WRITTEN BY:
MICKY NEILSON

ART AND COVER BY:
SEAN "CHEEKS" GALLOWAY

LETTERING BY:
SAIDA TEMOFONTE

Additional 'Behind the Scenes' Layouts by:
Sean "Cheeks" Galloway

Blizzard Special Thanks:
Chloe Fraboni, Allison Irons, Brie Messina,
Derek Rosenberg, Byron Parnell, and Anna Wan

WRITTEN BY: Micky Neilson

ARTIST: Sean "Cheeks" Galloway

GAME TEAM DIRECTION: Cameron Dayton, Sam Didier, Doug A. Gregory, Chris Metzen, Glenn Rane

LORE CONSULTATION: Madi Buckingham, Sean Copeland, Christi Kugler, Justin Parker, Anne Stickney

PRODUCTION: Chloe Fraboni, Allison Irons, Brianne Messina, Derek Rosenberg, Anna Wan

DIRECTOR, CONSUMER PRODUCTS: Byron Parnell

DIRECTORS, CREATIVE DEVELOPMENT: David Seeholzer

SPECIAL THANKS: Dario Brizuela, Table Taffy Studio's Derek Laufman, Hwang, Nguyen, Ryan Odagawa, DJ Welch, Caleb Sawyer

Published by Titan Books, London, in 2020.
Published by arrangement with Blizzard Entertainment, Inc., Irvine, California.

TITAN BOOKS

A division of Titan Publishing Group Ltd

144 Southwark Street

London SE1 0UP

www.titanbooks.com

Find us on Facebook: www.facebook.com/titanbooks

Follow us on Twitter: @TitanBooks

A CIP catalogue record for this title is available from the British Library.

ISBN: 9781789095739

Printed in China

CHAPTER ONE

The Song of Liu Lang

It is written, little cub, in the **Book of the Turtle...**

...that many years after the Sundering of the world, a young pandaren named Liu Lang looked out over the endless sea...

...and wondered what lay beyond the mists of our island home.

Caught up in the wanderlust, Liu Lang longed to explore.

Our ancestors dismissed his notions as whim and fancy, and they said if he left, he would surely become lost and never find his way back.

But Liu Lang's spirit was unshakable, and soon he departed upon the turtle Shen-zin Su...

Five years passed without word from Liu Lang, and he was thought by most to be gone forever. "See," they said, "that is what happens to adventure-seekers!"

But then, one day...

...he returned.

The rest of the world had survived the Sundering! Liu Lang spoke of amazing exploits, of a vast desert filled with trolls, of sights beyond belief. He prepared to set off again and asked if anyone would join him...

...and our forebears responded, "No, the world is too dangerous! Stay here with us, where you belong!"

Liu Lang would not stay. The open sea and the winding road called to him. And so he departed once more...

Another five years, and Liu Lang appeared once again. He had come to know a race of bull-people called tauren. He had seen more incredible and unbelievable things.

Upon the back of the turtle, he had built his home, but he had no one to share it with. Liu Lang asked if any of the women would join him on his adventures...

...but not one pandaren stepped forward.

And so Liu Lang set off alone.

He cast a final backward glance and spied a single vessel, a small boat, and on it...

...a lone, brave soul named Shinizi.

Shinizi and Liu Lang were happy, and they soon married. Together they set out on great adventures. Together they celebrated life.

The world had given much to them, and in time they gave to the world three beautiful cubs.

When Liu Lang arrived once more in Pandaria, he requested the aid of seven priests...

...hoping that they might lure elementals to the temple so that nature would continue to flourish on the back of Shen-zin Su.

Seeing all that had come to pass, seven powerful priests gathered their courage and agreed to join Liu Lang and Shinizi.

And so it was that the cycle repeated yet again...

Five years later the priests sought wives and husbands. Liu Lang had discovered a new continent!

At this time several of the most adventurous brewmasters joined a handful of other pandaren and made their home on the Great Turtle.

And from that day on, Liu Lang and the others returned home every five years. More and more pandaren chose to accompany them on their travels, until all of the boldest, most inquisitive of our kind had left the island.

When there were no pandaren left who would dare to join him, Liu Lang set out one final time...

It is said that soon after he left, Liu Lang reached his final destination in the journey of life.

The book tells us that he went to sleep beneath his umbrella and that his spirit became one with Shen-zin Su.

Atop a quiet hill in what we now call the Wood of Staves, the umbrella bloomed into a giant tree.

Shinizi kept Liu Lang's memory close to her heart, and she watched those around her prosper until the time came for her contented spirit to depart as well.

As for Shen-zin Su, the Great Turtle continued to grow and grow...

And grow!

He became known as the Wandering Isle, a continent unto himself, a home to generation after generation.

Yet over time those generations traveled less and less. They grew comfortable and complacent, and they forgot the lesson of Liu Lang.

The spark of wanderlust that had shone so brightly in their hearts faded.

When I came of age and the Traveler's Path called to me, I tried to inspire others to strike out as well, but they would not hear of it. They said I would become lost and never find my way home.

Sound familiar?

My own brother, your father, begged me to stay. But my yearning would not be denied.

And so one day I left and never looked back.

But I never forgot about you, little cub, and I never will.

Always remember, dear Li Li, life is an adventure. Live it to the fullest every day, and promise me you'll think of your old uncle once in a while. Love, Uncle Chen.

LIFE IS AN ADVENTURE. LIFE IS AN ADVENTURE...

LI LI STORMSTOUT!

I'VE BEEN LOOKING ALL OVER! YOU'RE SUPPOSED TO BE IN BED!

I AM IN BED, POP! WHAT YOU'RE SEEING IS A HALLUCINATION, A FIGMENT OF YOUR OVERACTIVE IMAGINATION, BROUGHT ON BY LACK OF SLEEP AND STRONG TEA. LOOK, I'LL PROVE IT--

SEE, SOLID OBJECTS PASS RIGHT THROUGH ME. NO BIG DEAL; SINCE I'M NOT REAL, YOU CAN JUST PRETEND THIS NEVER HAPPENED.

VERY FUNNY! I'VE TOLD YOU TIME AND AGAIN ABOUT COMING OUT HERE, BURYING YOUR HEAD IN THOSE BOOKS, LOSING YOURSELF IN MY BROTHER'S *DELUSIONS* OF *GRANDEUR!* THE *SPIRIT FESTIVAL* IS NEARLY UPON US, AND YOU HAVE A FULL DAY OF PREPARATION TOMORROW.

NOW, OFF YOU GO! IF YOU INSIST ON EMBRACING SILLY DREAMS, DO IT WHILE YOU SLEEP!

PANDOWAN! FOCUS! THE FIRST OF YOU TO DROP YOUR POTS WILL ANSWER TO ME!

I CAN THINK OF A THOUSAND THINGS I'D RATHER BE DOING WITH MY TIME. LITERALLY A THOUSAND.

PUT A CORK IN IT BEFORE YOU BRING STRONGBO OVER HERE!

HOW COULD YOU? I'VE NEVER BEEN SO EMBARRASSED IN MY LIFE! THE MOST IMPORTANT CELEBRATION OF THE YEAR!

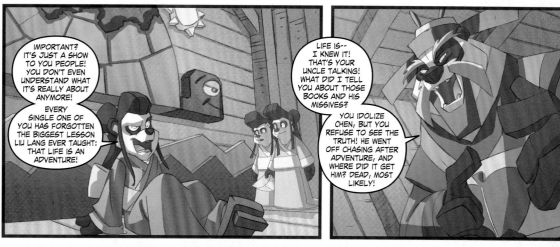

IMPORTANT? IT'S JUST A SHOW TO YOU PEOPLE! YOU DON'T EVEN UNDERSTAND WHAT IT'S REALLY ABOUT ANYMORE!

EVERY SINGLE ONE OF YOU HAS FORGOTTEN THE BIGGEST LESSON LIU LANG EVER TAUGHT: THAT LIFE IS AN ADVENTURE!

LIFE IS-- I KNEW IT! THAT'S YOUR UNCLE TALKING! WHAT DID I TELL YOU ABOUT THOSE BOOKS AND HIS MISSIVES?

YOU IDOLIZE CHEN, BUT YOU REFUSE TO SEE THE TRUTH! HE WENT OFF CHASING AFTER ADVENTURE, AND WHERE DID IT GET HIM? DEAD, MOST LIKELY!

HOW WOULD YOU KNOW? HOW WOULD ANY OF YOU? NO ONE EVER DARED TO GO AFTER HIM! YOUR OWN BROTHER, AND ALL YOU'VE DONE IS SIT AROUND LIKE THE REST, AFRAID OF THAT BIG SCARY WORLD OUT THERE!

THERE WAS A TIME WHEN ONLY THE BRAVEST PANDAREN MADE THEIR HOME ON SHEN-ZIN SU. NOW YOU'RE ALL NOTHING BUT...COWARDS!

ENOUGH! YOU ARE NEVER TO SET FOOT IN THE LIBRARY AGAIN! UNDERSTAND? *NEVER!*

NOW YOU *WILL* RETURN TO PRACTICE AND--LI LI! GET BACK HERE RIGHT NOW! DO YOU HEAR ME?

NOW!

CHAPTER TWO

Wanderlust

"THERE WE WAS ON THE HIGH SEAS, ME AND ME CREW, IN THE PROCESS O' RELIEVIN' A STORMWIND SHIP OF ITS CARGO..."

"HEY, WAIT A MINUTE-- YOU'RE A PIRATE!"

"PIRATE? NO. LIGHT, NO...I'M A PRIVATEER."

"OH."

"TOTALLY DIFFERENT. ANYWAYS, I LED THE CHARGE, O' COURSE, TAKIN' ON SIX OF THE BIGGEST SO'S ME MATES COULD--"

"ARE YOU TRYIN' TO PULL ONE OVER ON ME? I WON'T PAY FOR THE PINT IF YOU'RE GONNA BEND THE TRUTH!"

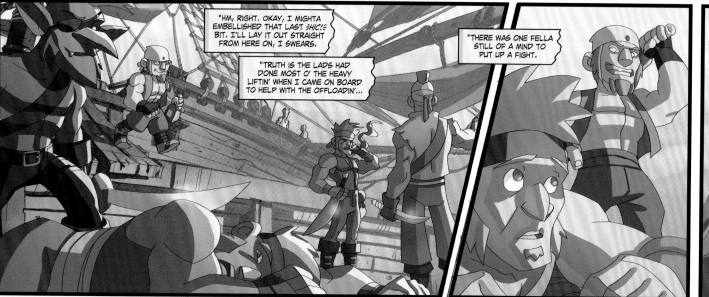

"HM, RIGHT. OKAY, I MIGHTA EMBELLISHED THAT LAST ≥HIC!≤ BIT. I'LL LAY IT OUT STRAIGHT FROM HERE ON, I SWEARS.

"TRUTH IS THE LADS HAD DONE MOST O' THE HEAVY LIFTIN' WHEN I CAME ON BOARD TO HELP WITH THE OFFLOADIN'...

"THERE WAS ONE FELLA STILL OF A MIND TO PUT UP A FIGHT.

"I USED A BIT O' ME PERSUASION AND CONVINCED 'IM TO COME QUIETLY.

"THEN I HEARD THE BOYS CALL OUT THAT THERE'S SOMETHIN' BELOWDECKS WE GOTTA SEE..."

"WOW! THAT'S AMAZING!! AND WHERE WERE *YOU* THIS WHOLE TIME?"

"WELL, YOU KNOW, I DON'T LOWER MESELF TO ≋HIC!≋ FISTICUFFS UNLESS THERE BE NO OTHER RECOURSE.

"THE CREW DECIDED TO FISH THEMSELVES OUTTA THE DRINK AND SEEK FORTUNE ELSEWHERE, BUT..."

"...WE DIDN'T ALL COME AWAY EMPTY-HANDED.

"YOUR UNCLE, HE GAVE ME A PARTIN' GIFT, SEE...

...I'LL TELL YA WHAT, THOUGH...

...IF YA CAN OPEN IT, I'LL GIVE YA HALF WHAT'S INSIDE. I NEVER COULD FIGURE OUT THE LOCK MESELF.

I SWEARS IT ON ME MAMMY'S WOODEN TEETH.

THIS WAS REALLY MY UNCLE'S?

THEN IT'S RIGHTFULLY MINE ANYWAY.

I TOLD YA YER UNCLE GIFTED IT TO ME!

AND WHAT'D I TELL YOU ABOUT LYING? GIVE IT TO ME NOW, AND *YOU* WON'T BE NEEDING WOODEN TEETH.

WELL, SEE HERE, I--

AND I'LL THROW IN ANOTHER PINT.

WE ≋HIC!≋ GOT US AN ACCORD.

"THUNDERBREW." I WONDER WHAT THAT MEANS.

YOU WON'T BE STAYING HERE LONG ENOUGH TO FIND OUT. WE'RE LEAVING.

DON'T BE SUCH A PAIN. SIT. HAVE SOME TEA.

I SAW YOUR FIRE ALL THE WAY FROM TOWN. IF I SAW IT, ANYONE CAN SEE IT. NOT EVERYONE AROUND HERE IS FRIENDLY, LI LI.

I FOUND A CLUE ABOUT UNCLE CHEN. CAN'T YOU JUST TELL POP YOU COULDN'T FIND ME?

YOUR FATHER IS WORRIED, ESPECIALLY AFTER WHAT HAPPENED TO YOUR MOTHER. EVEN THAT FISHERMAN, WANYO... BRINGING YOU HOME SAFELY IS MY SWORN DUTY.

DUTY, YEAH, BLAH BLAH. WANYO JUST GOT LOST. THERE'S NOTHING WE CAN DO ABOUT IT. NOTHING WE CAN DO ABOUT MY MOM EITHER. BUT WE CAN DO SOMETHING ABOUT UNCLE CHEN.

LOOK, SIT AND DRINK SOME TEA WITH ME, AND WE CAN LEAVE RIGHT AFTER. I PROMISE.

VERY WELL. ONE CUP, AND THEN WE GO.

AREN'T YOU THE LEAST BIT CURIOUS ABOUT WHAT HAPPENED TO CHEN?

WHY SHOULD I CARE ABOUT CHEN?

HE MENTIONED YOU IN HIS LETTERS. SAID YOU WERE FRIENDS.

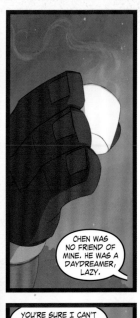

CHEN WAS NO FRIEND OF MINE. HE WAS A DAYDREAMER, LAZY.

YOU'RE SURE I CAN'T PERSUADE YOU TO STAY ANY LONGER?

CHAPTER THREE

Thunderbrew

STORMWIND CITY. CATHEDRAL OF LIGHT.

I DON'T SEE WHAT YOUR INTEREST IS IN THEIR RELIGION.

I'M INTERESTED IN ALL RELIGIONS.

THEY BELIEVE IN THE HOLY LIGHT. SAYS HERE THAT THE LIGHT SHINES ON EACH AND EVERY BEING ON AZEROTH.

PERHAPS WE CAN SHINE THE LIGHT ON THIS THUNDERBREW OF YOURS SO WE CAN LEAVE.

THUNDERBREW? AH YES, A FINE LAGER.

LAGER, HM? FIGURES.

I NEED TO FIND OUT MORE ABOUT THIS THUNDERBREW. DO YOU KNOW WHERE WE COULD GET SOME?

WHY, YES. AT BREWFEST. STARTED YESTERDAY.

THE DWARVES OF IRONFORGE PUT ON A SHOW THAT'S GUARANTEED TO SLUR THE SPEECH AND WOBBLE THE WALK.

OH, THAT SOUNDS AMAZING! WHAT'S THE QUICKEST WAY TO IRONFORGE?

THE DEEPRUN TRAM. DEPARTS FROM THE DWARVEN DISTRICT.

YAY! SOMEPLACE WE HAVEN'T BEEN YET! THANKS!

LIGHT BLESS YOU!

LI LI, I DON'T BELIEVE A BEER FESTIVAL IS THE BEST USE OF--

LESS TALKIN'; MORE WALKIN'!

SAYS IN ONE OF CHEN'S LETTERS THAT THE DEEPRUN TRAM WAS CONSTRUCTED BY THE GNOMES TO PROVIDE QUICK AND EFFICIENT TRANSPORT BETWEEN IRONFORGE AND STORMWIND.

HE SAYS IT'S THE MOST PRACTICAL THING THEY EVER BUILT!

FASCINATING.

RRRRRRRRR

Me granddad *Grimbooze* was busy workin' at his distillery in Kharanos when the stranger arrived.

Your uncle said he'd searched far and wide for the finest brews in the land, and in all that time, he'd heard **one name** over and over again: Thunderbrew!

So Chen, who claimed to be a fine brewer in his own right, had sought out me granddad to see if the tales were true.

Grimbooze agreed to let Chen try his lager as long as Chen would return the favor.

They sat down with each other's lager in front o' them, and together...

...they took their first sip...

NOT BAD. I MIGHT NEED A WEE BIT MORE TO MAKE AN HONEST ASSESSMENT.

I ALSO WISH TO CONTINUE SAMPLING.

Chen employed a strange and mystifyin' vessel he called the Jug o' a Thousand Cups. Indeed, there seemed to be no end to the quantity o' alcohol it could hold.

The "sampling" continued...

...and continued...

...and continued.

By the end, they'd drunk enough to drown a hydra.

They'd even drained the Jug o' a Thousand Cups.

GRIMBOOZE THUNDERBREW, I HAVE COME TO A... DECISION. I HEREBY DECLARE THAT YOURS IS THE BETTER BREW!

BRREP!

NAY, AFTER A GREAT DEAL O' ME OWN CONSIDERATION, I'VE COME TO THE CONCLUSION THAT *YOURS* BE THE BETTER BREW!

NO, NO, REALLY, I...I INSIST. YOURS IS BETTER.

YOURS, I SAY!

NO, YOURS.

YOURS.

YOURS.

YOURS.

YOURS, YOURS, YOURS.

WELL, AS MUCH AS I HATE TO SAY IT, THERE BE ONLY ONE WAY TO SETTLE THIS...

COME ONE, COME ALL, TO AN ALCOHOLIC TASTE-TESTING EXTRAVAGANZA! YOU -YES, YOU- MUST DECIDE WHICH IS BETTER: STORMSTOUT OR THUNDERBREW! BRING YOUR FRIENDS AND YOUR NEIGHBORS AND YOUR THIRST TO THE **FESTIVAL O' BREWS** JUST OUTSIDE IRONFORGE!

Chen whipped up a batch o' his finest, enough to besot an army o' Wildhammers...

STORMSTOUT

Not to be outdone, Grimbooze prepared a mountain o' kegs containin' his own special brew. Together they got set to face off, two groggy gladiators puttin' their life's work on the line. But...

THUNDERBREW

...there was another.

When he learned o' the contest, the Dark Iron dwarf Coren Direbrew insisted on bein' allowed to participate. He griped and whined and raised such a stink that Granddad Grimbooze finally gave in.

And so, the stage was set...

Keg after keg was consumed. Votes were cast and tallied...

...an' it became clear early on that Granddad Grimbooze and your uncle, Chen, were neck and neck. In fact, Coren had only received two votes, and one o' them was his!

POW

Coren was fit to be tied. Words were exchanged... and as ye may know, Dark Irons and the rest o' the clans don't exactly get on with each other anyway...

By his own admission, Granddad was knocked silly. But your uncle stood up in Grimbooze's defense...

CHAPTER FOUR

Kalimdor

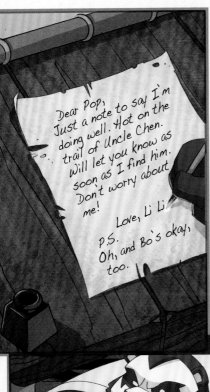

Dear Pop,
Just a note to say I'm doing well. Hot on the trail of Uncle Chen. Will let you know as soon as I find him. Don't worry about me!

Love, Li Li.
P.S. Oh, and Bo's okay, too.

SO... MISSING HOME?

NICE TRY.

IS IT REALLY SO DIFFICULT TO ADMIT? YOUR FATHER MISSES YOU, AND YOU MISS HIM...

WHATEVER PROBLEMS THE TWO OF YOU HAVE, YOU CAN'T SOLVE THEM BY RUNNING AWAY.

YOU KNOW, THE MORE YOU PRETEND THIS IS ABOUT ME, THE MORE I REALIZE IT ISN'T.

AND WHAT DOES THAT MEAN?

IT'S ABOUT CHEN AND WHATEVER HAPPENED BETWEEN YOU TWO, RIGHT?

IS THAT REALLY SO DIFFICULT TO ADMIT?

"≈SIGH≈ YOUR UNCLE AND I, WE WERE THE GREATEST OF FRIENDS. WE TRAINED TOGETHER EVERY DAY. WE WERE THE TOP PANDOWAN STUDENTS, BUT OUR STYLES WERE VERY DIFFERENT...

"...YOUR UNCLE PLAYED FAST AND LOOSE. HE WAS UNORTHODOX, ELUSIVE, UNPREDICTABLE... BUT EFFECTIVE. ATTUNED TO STORM, EARTH, AND FIRE. MANY CONSIDERED HIM THE BEST.

"AS FOR ME, I ALWAYS PREFERRED THE DIRECT APPROACH. I FOCUSED MY ATTUNEMENT ON EARTH...

"STRONG.

"STEADY.

"UNYIELDING.

WE BOTH KNEW THAT SOMEDAY WE WOULD FACE EACH OTHER TO DETERMINE WHO WAS NUMBER ONE--WHO WOULD BECOME THE GEOMASTER, TRAINER OF THE GREAT TURTLE'S YOUNG PANDOWAN.

YOUR UNCLE BECAME INCREASINGLY RESTLESS. HE SPOKE OF THE WANDERLUST, HOW IT HAD BEEN FAR TOO LONG SINCE ANYONE HAD GONE TO SEEK THE OUTSIDE WORLD; TO EXPLORE IT AND UNDERGO FANTASTIC ADVENTURES.

HE WANTED ALSO TO DISCOVER EXOTIC INGREDIENTS FOR HIS BREWS AND TEAS.

"WHEN YOU CAME INTO THE WORLD, CHEN TOOK TO YOU IMMEDIATELY. HE SPENT MANY NIGHTS FILLING YOUR HEAD WITH HIS OUTLANDISH NOTIONS.

"YEARS PASSED, AND AS THE TIME OF OUR CHALLENGE GREW NEAR, I BECAME FRUSTRATED WITH CHEN'S CONSTANT DAYDREAMING."

"I TOLD HIM WHAT YEARS OF ADVENTURING HAD TAUGHT OUR ANCESTORS: THAT THERE WAS NOTHING IN THE OUTSIDE WORLD THAT WE COULDN'T FIND RIGHT THERE AT HOME.

"I TRIED TO TELL HIM THAT THE MOST IMPORTANT THINGS WERE THERE IN FRONT OF HIM, BUT HE WOULDN'T LISTEN. THE TWO OF US ARGUED...

"...AND WHEN THE DAY OF OUR FINAL TEST CAME, YOUR UNCLE HAD LEFT. HE LEFT ME ALONE... TO PURSUE HIS DELUSIONAL FANTASIES."

AND?

AND WHAT? YOU WANTED TO KNOW WHAT HAPPENED BETWEEN US. I TOLD YOU.

THAT'S IT? THAT'S WHY YOU'RE SO UPTIGHT? BECAUSE YOU DIDN'T GET A CHANCE TO PROVE HOW TOUGH YOU WERE? YOU GOTTA BE KIDDING ME!

I NEVER EXPECTED YOU TO UNDERSTAND. IT'S WHY I DIDN'T SHARE THE STORY BEFORE.

WELL, YOU WERE RIGHT: I DON'T UNDERSTAND.

YOUR RAM IS NUZZLING ME.

THAT'S NOTHING COMPARED TO WHAT YOUR RAM'S DOING RIGHT NOW.

WHAT-- HEY!

SO THAT'S WHY THEY CALL IT A POOP DECK!

YES, I HEAR YOU.

CRASH

IF WE LOSE THEM, ZHAHARA WILL NOT. AND EVEN IF THEY EVADE HER, THEIR KIND IS RARE. THEY DRAW ATTENTION.

I SUPPOSE. THE DWARVES WOULDN'T SHUT UP ABOUT THE ONE THEY CALLED BO.

SO YOU SAID. A FIGHTER WHOSE LIKE THEY HAD NEVER SEEN... A WORTHY CHALLENGE. I LOOK FORWARD TO FACING HIM IN COMBAT.

PERHAPS AT LAST I WILL EXPERIENCE THE *BREATH* OF *ETERNITY*.

THE WHAT OF WHAT?

ZHAHARA SEEKS THE *PEARL*, BUT I SEEK SOMETHING DIFFERENT. THERE IS A MOMENT, YOU SEE, WHEN TWO OPPONENTS FACE EACH OTHER, WHEN THEY ARE EVENLY MATCHED...

...A QUIET MOMENT IN THE MIDST OF BATTLE, WHEN ONE WARRIOR STARES INTO THE EYES OF THE OTHER, MENTALLY EXECUTING A HUNDRED TECHNIQUES, EXPLORING COUNTLESS SCENARIOS, UNTOLD OUTCOMES.

IT IS SAID THAT A LIFETIME IS FOUGHT IN THAT SINGLE MOMENT, A BREATH OF ETERNITY. I LIVE FOR THAT INSTANT. I HAVE YET TO FIND IT.

AND YOUR STUPIDITY COULD COST ME MY CHANCE. SHOULD AN INCIDENT LIKE THE DEEPRUN TRAM HAPPEN AGAIN, I'LL SKIN YOU ALIVE.

OH YEAH? WELL, THE WAY I SEE IT, I'M UP HERE AND YOU'RE DOWN THERE. SO WHY DON'T YOU TAKE YOUR THREATS AND--

URK!

SKIN YOU ALIVE, AND FEED WHAT'S LEFT TO THIS BRAIN-DEAD OGRE OF YOURS.

SEE, MY PROBLEM IS I TALK TOO MUCH, AND PEOPLE CAN'T ALWAYS TELL WHEN I'M KIDDING. I'VE BEEN TOLD I'M UNREADABLE.

NO NEED FOR HOSTILITY, CHIEF. HOW 'BOUT WE LET BYGONES BE BYGONES?

ZHAHARA SEES SOMETHING IN YOU, SO YOU LIVE...

...FOR NOW. DON'T INTERRUPT MY MEDITATIONS AGAIN.

THERE'S A NICE OPEN SPOT IN A PLACE CALLED WINDSHEAR CRAG. THE VENTURE COMPANY CLEARED OUT ALL THE FOREST THERE.

WHO?

A GOBLIN-RUN ORGANIZATION, PART OF A BIG TRADE COALITION. THEY, UH... SPECIALIZE IN NATURAL RESOURCES.

PARASITES, IN OTHER WORDS. LEECHES DRAINING THE WORLD OF ITS LIFEBLOOD.

THEY CALL THEMSELVES ENTREPRENEURS.

I CALL THEM A DISEASE.

HEY, WHADDYA WANT FROM ME? I JUST FLY ZEPPELINS.

OH, LOOK...

"...WE'RE HERE."

THE MORE I SEE OF THIS WONDERFUL WORLD OF YOURS, THE MORE I DETEST IT.

OKAY, SO, YEAH, IT'S NOT ALL ROSES. THE GOBLINS DID A TERRIBLE THING HERE, BUT THERE'S NOTHING WE CAN DO ABOUT IT NOW.

THIS HIDDEN VALLEY ISN'T GONNA FIND ITSELF. COME ON, RAM; LET'S MAKE TRACKS!

AANY DAY NOW. HYA! GO! GO GET 'EM!

WHAT GIVES? YOU CAN'T BE TIRED; YOU HAVEN'T TAKEN US ANYWHERE YET! COME ON, TALK TO ME... WHAT'S IT GONNA TAKE TO GET YOU TO MOVE?

WHAT DOES IT MATTER? ENDLESS MILES OF MOUNTAINS TO EXPLORE IN SEARCH OF A PLACE WE DON'T KNOW THE LOCATION OF, A PLACE THAT MAY NOT EVEN EXIST.

OR HADN'T YOU THOUGHT OF THAT?

YOU'RE ALWAYS SO SURE THAT YOU'RE RIGHT. DON'T THINK FOR ONE MINUTE I'M STUPID, MASTER "ATTUNED TO THE EARTH..."

...I MIGHT NOT KNOW THE LOCATION, BUT I'LL BET YOU CAN TALK TO THE EARTH AND FIND IT.

AND WHY SHOULD I, LITTLE ONE? TO MAKE THINGS EASY FOR YOU? BECAUSE IT'S WHAT YOU WANT? HOW MANY TIMES DO I HAVE TO TELL YOU, YOU CAN'T ALWAYS TAKE THE EASY WAY? YOU CAN'T ALWAYS GET WHAT YOU WANT.

NO, BECAUSE THE SOONER I FIND CHEN, THE SOONER YOU CAN TAKE ME BACK TO POP. IT'S A WIN FOR BOTH OF US. SO, HAVE A LITTLE HEART-TO-HEART. OR HEART-TO-ROCK, OR HOWEVER THAT WORKS, AND I'LL GET OUR STUBBORN FRIENDS HERE TO MOVE.

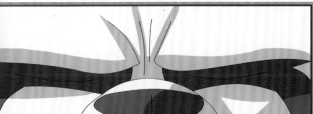

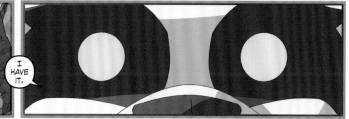

"YOU SURE YOU'RE DOING THIS RIGHT?"

"I WATCHED CHEN DO IT A HUNDRED TIMES!"

"WORT IS WHAT YOU GET AFTER YOU MIX YOUR GRIST AND YOUR WATER IN A PROCESS CALLED MASHING.

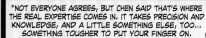

"NOT EVERYONE AGREES, BUT CHEN SAID THAT'S WHERE THE REAL EXPERTISE COMES IN. IT TAKES PRECISION AND KNOWLEDGE, AND A LITTLE SOMETHING ELSE, TOO... SOMETHING TOUGHER TO PUT YOUR FINGER ON.

"INSTINCT, I GUESS. TEA, BEER, DOESN'T MATTER. EITHER YOU'RE BORN WITH THE INSTINCT OR YOU'RE NOT. BREWMASTERS ARE BORN WITH IT. CHEN WAS, AND I'M GONNA PROVE THAT I WAS TOO!

"NEXT YOU THROW IN THE HOPS, AND THAT'S WHERE YOUR BEER GETS ITS ATTITUDE! FLAVOR, AROMA, BITTERNESS. THEN IT'S TIME FOR YEAST. TIME FOR FERMENTATION.

"CHEN TAUGHT ME SPECIAL TECHNIQUES HANDED DOWN FROM GENERATION TO GENERATION...WAYS TO SPEED FERMENTATION AND ENHANCE FLAVOR!

SOME CONDITIONING AND FILTERING, A LITTLE MORE TIME, AND FINALLY, THE MOMENT OF TRUTH. YOU COME TO THE END.

CHEN ALWAYS SAID YOU HOPE FOR PERFECTION, BUT NO MATTER WHAT, YOU REALIZE HOW MEMORABLE AND REWARDING THE JOURNEY TO GET THERE WAS.

NO MATTER WHAT.

WHAT IF AZSHARA REALLY IS CURSED? WHAT IF THIS IS WHERE CHEN'S JOURNEY ENDED... FOREVER?

DON'T TALK LIKE THAT! I DIDN'T COME THIS FAR TO LET YOUR THUNDER-CLOUD POUR ALL OVER ME! HAVEN'T YOU EVER THOUGHT ABOUT OUR FINDING ALL THESE CLUES, RUNNING INTO THESE PEOPLE WHO KNEW UNCLE CHEN... THAT IT'S MORE THAN JUST A COINCIDENCE?

WHAT ARE YOU TRYING TO SAY?

I THINK WE'RE DESTINED TO FIND CHEN. I THINK HE WANTS TO BE FOUND! HE KNEW I'D COME LOOKING FOR HIM, AND THESE CLUES ARE HIS MESSAGES TO ME, LIKE HIS LETTERS.

RUUUUUMBLEEE

THE CHEST WAS TAKEN TO A ROYAL VAULT...

THERE SHOULD BE A STAIRCASE...

...UNDER ALL THIS.

DO THE HONORS?

HOW MANY TIMES DO I HAVE TO TELL YOU--

I KNOW, I KNOW. I CAN'T ALWAYS TAKE THE EASY WAY. LOOK, THE FIRST HUNDRED TIMES YOU SAID IT HAVEN'T SUNK IN; WHAT DIFFERENCE WILL ONE MORE MAKE?

FINE. HAVE IT YOUR WAY, THEN, AS YOU ALWAYS DO. BUT THIS IS IT...

ONE...

...LAST...

...TIME!

KOOM!

DOESN'T LOOK LIKE THERE'S MUCH LEFT...

THERE IT IS!

CAN YOU BELIEVE IT'S STILL HERE?

NOT SURPRISING, CONSIDERING WHAT'S INSIDE. IT'S NOT EVEN LOCKED.

PFOO

YES, BUT IT'S--

CHAPTER FIVE

Journey's End

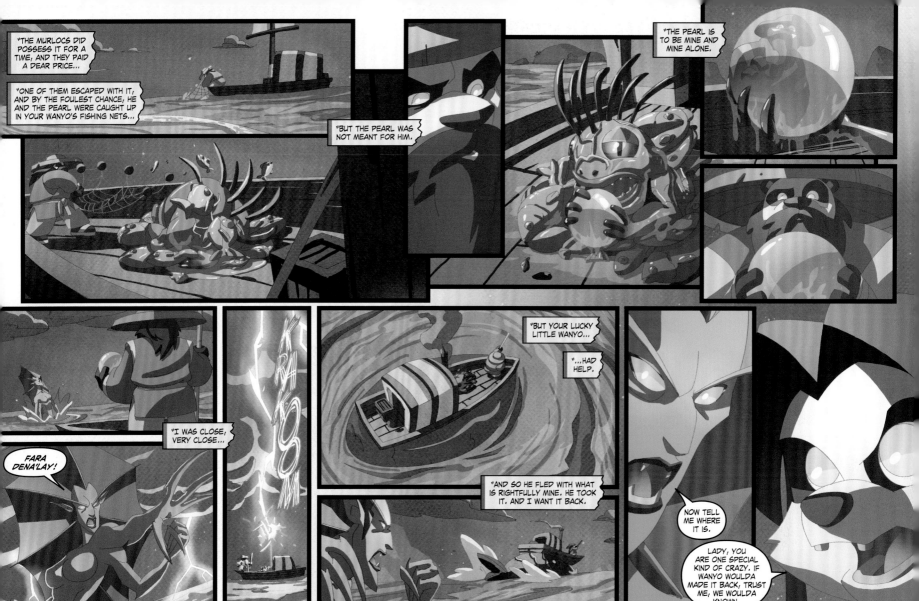

I SEARCHED MILES IN EVERY DIRECTION AND NEVER FOUND ANY WRECKAGE. WHICH MEANS YOU'RE LYING. WHICH MEANS YOU *KNOW* WHERE IT IS.

TELL ME NOW, OR I'LL HUNT DOWN YOUR PRECIOUS TURTLE AND GUT IT. LET THE SHARKS HAVE A FEEDING FRENZY. YOUR BELOVED HOME CAN JOIN US AT THE BOTTOM OF THE OCEAN!

OH, I FORGOT...YOUR PEOPLE CAN'T BREATHE UNDER-WATER, CAN THEY?

TELL ME WHAT I WANT TO KNOW, AND PERHAPS YOU WON'T HAVE TO DIE.

YOU ARE ONE SERIOUSLY WARPED OLD HAG, YOU KNOW THAT? BESIDES...SOMETHING TELLS ME, IF YOU COULD HAVE FOUND THE TURTLE, YOU WOULD HAVE DONE IT BY NOW.

SUCH A CLEVER LITTLE GIRL, YOU *WILL* TELL ME WHERE TO FIND THE PEARL. *AND* THE TURTLE. IF NOT...WELL, WE HAVE SEVERAL METHODS OF MOTIVATION.

ARE YOU CERTAIN THE OTHER ONE WILL FIND THE MAP?

HE WON'T MISS IT. CARVED ON A STONE TABLET WITH A SINGLE MESSAGE: "COME ALONE, OR THE LITTLE ONE DIES." HE'LL BE HERE. AND I'LL BE READY.

KEEP THE CUB DRUGGED ENOUGH SO SHE CANNOT USE HER ABILITIES. STAY FOCUSED.

AND YOUR SUPERIORS? YOU'RE SURE THEY DON'T KNOW OF THE PEARL?

I'M SURE. THEY'RE TOO BUSY WITH THEIR FANTASIES OF A PANDAREN HOMELAND.

GOOD.

HOW FORMIDABLE WE ARE...AND HOW UNCONQUERABLE WE SHALL BE.

SHE CHAINED UP GOOD.

THAT OLD WITCH IS CRAZY. IT'S NOT TOO LATE TO STOP HER, THOUGH.

STOP HER? WHY? I HAVE IT ON GOOD AUTHORITY THAT YOUR LIBRARY HOUSES SOME OF THE RAREST AND MOST ANCIENT ALCHEMICAL TEXTS...YOU GUYS KNOW ABOUT STUFF NO ONE ELSE HAS EVER SEEN!

AND ZHAHARA SAID SHE'LL GIVE ME FIRST CRACK AT IT! ALL OF IT!

AND YOU BELIEVE HER? NOT ONLY THAT, BUT DID YOU EVER THINK ABOUT JUST *ASKING* IF YOU COULD SEE THE TEXTS?

SILENCE!

YOUR COMPANION WILL COME FOR ME ON THE OTHER ISLAND. WHEN HE DOES, I'LL FIGHT HIM TO THE DEATH. YOU'LL BE WATCHING.

GIVE HER THE SPYGLASS.

YOU CAN STOP THE FIGHT AT ANY TIME BY TELLING US WHAT WE WANT TO KNOW. TELL BLOKK TO GIVE THE SIGNAL. IF YOU DON'T...

I'LL RELIEVE YOUR FRIEND OF THE BURDEN ON HIS SHOULDERS.

GOBLIN! TIME TO LIGHT THE FIRE!

SLAP

SSSHZZZZZSSSSHHZZ

SSSHHZZZZIING

COME ON, COME ON...

VWUP VWUP VWUP VWUP

HA! HA! HA!

MM.

CHEN...
...LONG HAVE I WAITED FOR THIS DAY. I HAVE DEDICATED MY LIFE IN TRAINING SO I MIGHT DEFEAT THE ONLY BEING WHO HAS EVER DEFEATED ME.

ZHAHARA! YOU STAY OUT OF THIS! I NEED NO ASSISTANCE.

MY BLADE...

...SEEKS VENGEANCE!!

RRAAGH!

GLUG
GLUG
GLUG

PFOO!

FWOOSH

AH, AH--

TAKE ME OVER... BY THE ROCKS.

FWUMP

I SEE YOU'VE AGED LIKE BEER.

AND YOU'VE GOTTEN UGLIER!

HA! LI LI! GIVE US A MOMENT...

ALL THIS TIME, CHEN, I HARBORED ANGER. RESENTMENT TOWARD YOU FOR LEAVING ME.

NONE OF THAT MATTERS NOW.

LISTEN. I'VE SEEN WHAT ANGER AND RESENTMENT CAN LEAD TO IF LEFT UNCHECKED.

THE TRUTH IS, PART OF ME WAS JEALOUS; PART OF ME KNEW JUST HOW... GOOD YOU REALLY WERE. YOU WERE ALWAYS... EXTRAORDINARY.

AND YOU WERE ALWAYS INVINCIBLE.

NOT... TODAY.

I DON'T HAVE...MUCH TIME LEFT. I WANT YO TO TAKE LI LI. I DON'T WANT HER TO SEE.

COME HERE, LITTLE ONE!

YOU MUST RETURN HOME NOW WITH CHEN...NO ARGUMENT! TELL YOUR FATHER ALL THAT HAS HAPPENED.

NO. I WILL REMAIN HERE.

BUT YOU'RE COMING WITH US.

I DON'T WANNA GO!

HOW MANY TIMES DO I HAVE TO TELL YOU...?

YOU CAN'T ALWAYS GET WHAT YOU WANT.

IF I HADN'T BROUGHT YOU HERE, IF I HADN'T LEFT HOME...THIS IS ALL MY FAULT.

LISTEN VERY CAREFULLY... ...EVERY CHOICE I MADE, I MADE ON MY OWN.

I THOUGHT I KNEW SO MUCH...BUT YOU'VE GIVEN ME THE GREATEST GIFT OF ALL: THE GIFT OF ENLIGHTENMENT. IF I COULD DO IT ALL AGAIN, I WOULD.

IT HAS BEEN MY HONOR...TO SHARE THIS ADVENTURE WITH YOU.

I DON'T-- I CAN'T...

DON'T YOU CRY, LITTLE ONE. ALL IS WELL NOW. DON'T CRY.

I WISH TO STAY AND WATCH THE SUNRISE. THE SAME SUN THAT SHINES ON EACH AND EVERY BEING ON AZEROTH...NOT JUST SHEN-ZIN SU.

NOW YOU MUST GO! QUICKLY!

I KNOW THIS IS DIFFICULT. PERHAPS THE MOST DIFFICULT THING YOU WILL EVER DO. BUT WE DO IT FOR HIM. SO HE MAY SPEND HIS FINAL MOMENTS...

...IN PEACE AND DIGNITY.

SO...

...BEAUTIFUL.

Behind the Scenes of
World of Warcraft: Pearl of Pandaria

with artist
Sean "Cheeks" Galloway

Early Deeprun Tram/Dwarven District page layout.

Deeprun Tram sequence, page layout.

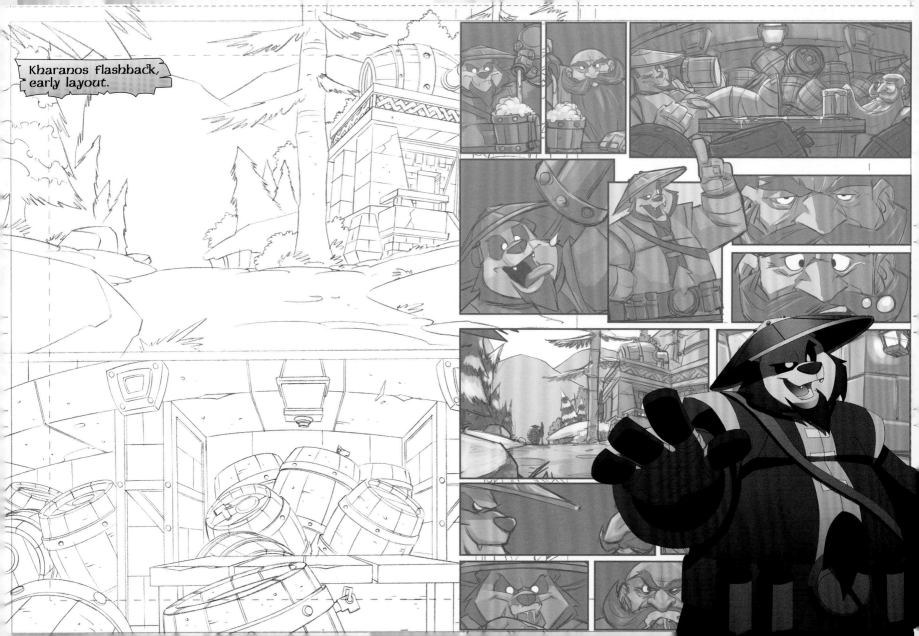

Kharanos flashback,
early layout.

Windshear Crag, layout and color.

PAGE 51 FIRST PASS

PAGE 52 FIRST PASS

PAGE 53 FIRST PASS

Early Rahjak
Design concept.

LIVE AREA

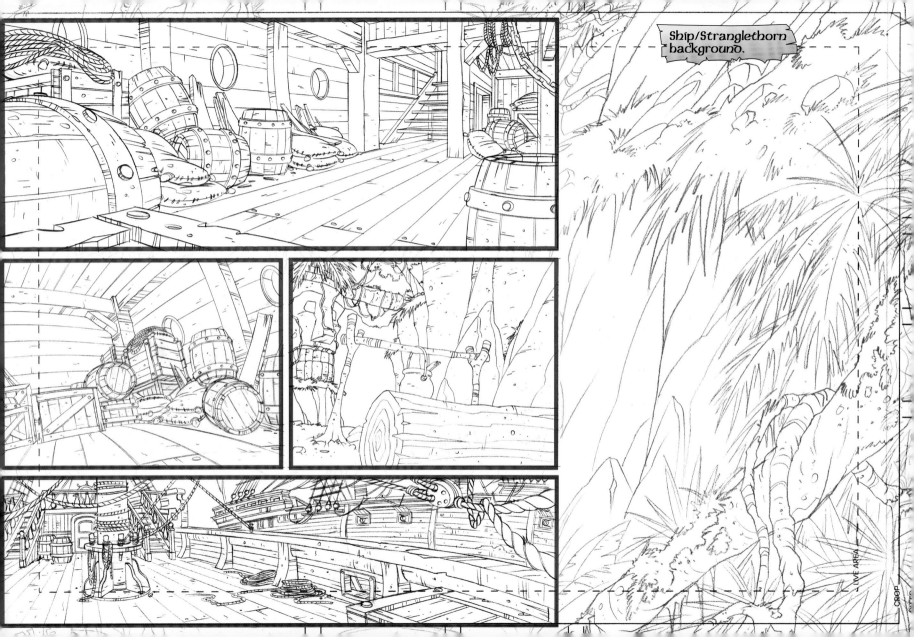

Ship/Stranglethorn background.

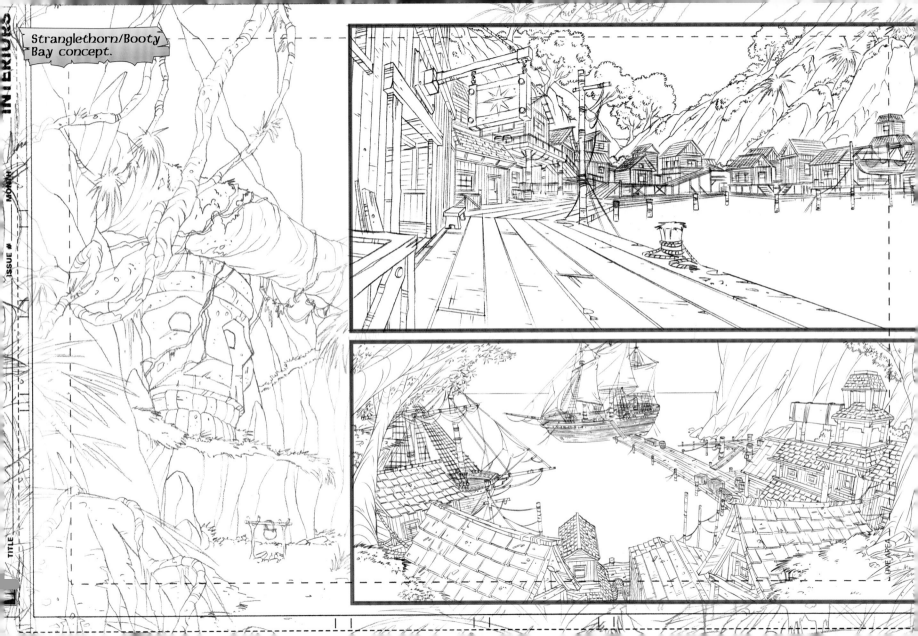

Stranglethorn/Booty
Bay concept.

Cover progression A.

Cover progression B.

Character designs for Bo, Chon Po, Li Li, Chen and Rahjak. Bo's sword was later changed to a staff.